1-08

6/12 OX

CR

— CONTINENTS —
NORTH AMERICA

Erinn Banting

WEIGL PUBLISHERS INC.

Published by Weigl Publishers Inc.
350 5th Avenue, Suite 3304, PMB 6G
New York, NY USA 10118-0069
Web site: www.weigl.com

Library of Congress Cataloging-in-Publication Data

Banting, Erinn.
  North America / Erinn Banting.
     p. cm. -- (Continents)
  Includes index.
  ISBN 1-59036-321-3 (hard cover : alk. paper) -- ISBN 1-59036-328-0 (soft cover : alk. paper)
  1. North America--Juvenile literature. I. Title. II. Continents (New York, N.Y.)
  G863.A75 2005
  919.8'904--dc22

                                                    2005003923

Printed in the United States of America
1 2 3 4 5 6 7 8 9 10 09 08 07 06 05

All of the Internet URLs given in the book were valid at the time of publication. However, due to the dynamic nature of the Internet, some addresses may have changed, or sites may have ceased to exist since publication. While the author and publisher regret any inconvenience this may cause readers, no responsibility for any such changes can be accepted by either the author or the publisher.

Project Coordinator
Heather C. Hudak

Copy Editor
Heather Kissock

Designer
Terry Paulhus

Layout
Gregg Muller
Kathryn Livingstone

Photo Researcher
Kim Winiski

Photograph Credits
Every reasonable effort has been made to trace ownership and to obtain permission to reprint copyright material. The publishers would be pleased to have any errors or omissions brought to their attention so that they may be corrected in subsequent printings.

Cover: Canada's Lake Louise is part of Banff National Park, Canada's first National Park and a UNESCO World Heritage Site. (Photographer's Choice/Alan Kearney/ Getty Images)

Credits: Getty Images: pages 1 (National Geographic/Rich Reid), 4-5 (National Geographic/David Edwards), 6L (Taxi/Gail Shumway), 6TR (Photographer's Choice/Moritz Steiger), 6BR (Taxi/Charles Benes), 8 (Stone/Jean Pragen), 9 (Robert Harding World Imagery/Gavin Hellier), 10 (Stone/Tim Flach), 11L (National Geographic/Joel Sartore), 11R (Taxi/Lester Lefkowitz), 12 (Image100), 13 (Taxi/Peter Adams), 14L (Taxi/Sandro Miller), 14R (National Geographic/Joe Raedle), 15 (Taxi/Benelux Press), 16 (Taxi/Peter Gridley), 17T (Time Life Pictures/Mansell/Time Life Pictures), 17B (Stock Montage), 18 (Hulton Archive/MPI), 19 (Hulton Archive), 20 (Imagebank/Walter Bibikow), 21 (Stone/Randy Wells), 22 (Imagebank/Walter Bibikow), 23L (David McNew), 23R (Stone/Robert Frerck), 24 (Time Life Pictures/Francois Lochon), 25T (AFP/Jim Watson), 25B (Frank Micelotta), 26 (Brian Bahr), 27 (Jeff Vinnick), 28T (Stone/William S. Helsel), 28B (Altrendo), 29T (Keam Collection), 29B (Hulton Archive/MPI), 30 (Imagebank/Tom Walker).

– CONTINENTS –
NORTH AMERICA

TABLE OF CONTENTS

Introduction

*N*amed after Italian explorer Amerigo Vespucci, who first landed on its shores in 1497, North America is one of the most **diverse** continents on Earth. From its arctic north to tropical south, North America is home to many different landscapes, wildlife, natural resources, climates, and cultures.

Stretching from the Grand Canyon to the Petrified Forest National Park, the Painted Desert covers 93,533 acres (37,851 hectares) of the United States. The desert is named for its colorful rock formations.

Before Europeans arrived in North America, Native Peoples lived off the land. They hunted in its forests and plains, grew corn in its fertile soil, gathered berries, and fished in its lakes and rivers. In the 1500s and 1600s, Europeans from England, France, and Spain began to **colonize** the continent. Those settlements grew into the countries we know today.

The continent of North America is divided into twenty-three independent nations. The three largest North American countries are the United States, Canada, and Mexico. Canada and the United States are also the second- and third-largest countries in the world respectively.

The cultures of the people who live in North America are as wide-ranging as the landscapes. The United States and Canada are multicultural countries, which means that their populations include people from around the world. People with European, Asian, and Middle Eastern backgrounds brought their foods, traditions, and religions to North America.

The history of North America also reflects the diversity of the land, the people, and the culture of the continent, making it one of the most interesting and varied places on Earth.

North America

North America stretches from the far north of the globe to a location near the **equator**. It is surrounded by the Atlantic Ocean on its east coast and the Pacific Ocean on its west coast. The Arctic Ocean is north of the continent. North America becomes very narrow at its southernmost point. This narrow stretch of land, called the Isthmus of Panama, links Central America to South America.

Besides Canada, Mexico, and the United States, North America also includes the West Indies and the Central American countries of Belize, Costa Rica, El Salvador, Guatemala, Honduras, Nicaragua, and Panama. Numerous small islands in the far north, off the east and west coasts, and in the Caribbean Sea are also considered to be part of North America.

Coyotes live in forests, prairies, mountains, chaparrals, and deserts throughout North America.

Fast Facts

While Mexico is part of North America, the culture of Mexico is similar to that of Latin American countries in South America.

Lake Superior, in central North America, is the continent's largest lake.

North America Continent Map

Location and Resources

Land and Climate

North America is the third-largest continent in the world. It covers about 9,450,000 square miles (24,474,000 square kilometers). North America's large size means it has very diverse landscapes and climates. Canada is the largest country in North America, with an area of almost 4,000,000 square miles (10,000,000 sq km). St. Christopher and Nevis, consisting of two islands in the Caribbean, is the smallest country, with an area of 101 square miles (261 sq km).

The northernmost parts of the United States, Canada, and Greenland are in an area called the Arctic Circle. Located near the North Pole, the weather in this region is extremely cold. Winters are very long, and the land is often buried under snow and ice. The southernmost parts of North America, which include Mexico, Central America, and the Caribbean Islands, are near the equator. These areas have long, warm summers, and short winters. There is rarely any snow, and the Sun shines for most of the year.

North America also includes Greenland, the largest island in the world. Kulusuk, an Inuit village, is located in Tunu, Greenland. Tunu means "the land at the back."

North America is divided into five geographical regions. In the north is the arctic/subarctic region. Few trees grow in the area, and the temperature is cold for most of the year. In eastern Canada, an area known as the Canadian Shield covers much of the land with thick forests. The Canadian Shield contains rough, rolling land and has a cool climate. A large, flat plain runs through the central part of the continent. This land is ideal for farming. Crops such as wheat and corn are grown here. Two mountain ranges border the continent. The steep Rocky Mountains run along the western coast, and the sloped Appalachians are located on the eastern coast.

Fast Facts

The tallest peak in North America is Mount McKinley, in the U.S. state of Alaska. The peak, located in Denali National Park, is 20,320 feet (6,194 meters) high.

The lowest point in North America is Badwater, a deep pool in Death Valley National Park, in the state of California. The pool is 282 feet (86 m) below sea level.

The longest river in North America is the Mississippi. It runs 2,340 miles (3,770 kilometers) from the state of Minnesota to the Gulf of Mexico. The river's name comes from an **Algonquin** word meaning "big water."

St. Lucia in the Caribbean is home to the Pitons, twin coastal peaks. The Pitons stand 2,000 feet (610 m) above sea level.

Plants and Animals

North America is home to a variety of plants and animals. Due to the wide range of landscapes and climates found in North America, many of these plants and animals are unique to the part of the continent in which they live.

Few plants grow in North America's arctic/subarctic region. Grasses, rushes, sedges, mosses, and lichens cling to the rocky and frozen ground. Stretching across most of southern and central Canada and into Alaska are fertile **boreal** forests. Trees such as spruce, fir, hemlock, and larch grow in these areas. **Deciduous** trees, such as the yellow pine, thrive in the southeast United States. Redwood and giant sequoia trees grow in California's mountains. In the rain forests of Mexico, palm trees reach toward the sky. They shelter hundreds of species of colorful flowers, ferns, and other plants that grow in the damp soil below.

Black bears, beavers, rabbits, caribou, deer, fox, and squirrels live throughout the North American interior. Polar bears live in the far northern areas. These bears have thick, warm fur and a layer of fat that allows them to swim in arctic waters.

Ducks, geese, loons, chickadees, robins, and cardinals are just some of the birds found in North America. Snakes, lizards, frogs, and other reptiles and amphibians can be found in the warmer regions of Canada, the United States and Mexico, as well as many of the continent's tropical islands.

Gila monsters live in the desert areas of Mexico and the southwestern United States.

Fast Facts

Less than 10 percent of the world is covered by rain forests. However, they are home to nearly half of the world's plant and animal species.

The heaviest weight ever recorded for a polar bear was 1,760 pounds (800 kilograms).

The beaver is one of Canada's national symbols. From the 1500s to the 1800s, people from Europe came to Canada to trap beavers, which they used to make fur hats.

Natural Resources

*M*inerals, water, and forests are some of the most important natural resources in North America. The continent is rich in natural resources, and the economies of the major countries depend on them as a source of income. Minerals are mined in Canada, the United States, and Mexico. The United States has rich deposits of coal in the Appalachian Mountain region. Iron ore is found in abundance in the United States near Lake Superior. It is also mined in the eastern provinces of Ontario, Quebec, and Newfoundland and Labrador in Canada. Oil is found in all three major countries.

Water is an important natural resource in North America. Hydroelectricity is created by damming the continent's numerous lakes and rivers. The countries use hydroelectricity to **generate** power.

Forests make up much of the Canadian provinces of British Columbia, Ontario, and Quebec. The western United States, including Washington, Oregon, California, and parts of the southeastern United States also have strong abundant tree coverage. Trees can be used in a variety of industries. Lumber is one of North America's largest exports.

Fast Facts

The United States is the largest producer of natural gas in the world.

The most important natural resource in Greenland is fish.

Uranium was such an important resource in the Northwest Territories, Canada, that one of its cities was named Uranium City.

Bauxite, a mineral used to make aluminum, is plentiful in parts of the Caribbean, such as the island of Jamaica.

Canada has 344,080 square miles (891,163 sq km) of water, which is more than any other country in the world. The largest inland body of water in Canada is Hudson Bay.

The Great Lakes, which are comprised of Lake Superior, Lake Huron, Lake Erie, Lake Ontario, and Lake Michigan, are located along the border of Canada and the United States. Lake Michigan is the only Great Lake located entirely in the United States.

The Glen Canyon Dam on the Colorado River in Arizona opened in 1966.

Canada's forests account for 15 percent of the world's softwood timber. The country produces 11 percent of the world's lumber.

Economy

Tourism

From hiking the tallest peaks of the Rocky Mountains to **SCUBA** diving in the warm waters of the Caribbean Sea, North America draws millions of tourists from around the world.

People visit Canada to hike, ski, and snowboard in the Rocky Mountains. They swim, canoe, and fish in the waters of the five Great Lakes. They visit the country's museums, theaters, and galleries to experience the culture of the land. Many tourists journey to the province of Quebec, which is home to a **bilingual** culture. People come to Quebec to experience both English and French language, culture, and food.

SCUBA diving is a popular tourist activity in Mexico and the Caribbean. Tour operators offer underwater adventures around Aruba, the Bahamas, the Barbados, St. Lucia, and many other islands.

One of the most popular tourist destinations in the United States is Grand Canyon National Park in Arizona. The park is home to the Grand Canyon, a 5,000-foot (1,500-m) deep canyon. Many people also visit the busy cities of the United States. In New York City, people enjoy musicals on a well-known street called Broadway. Visitors to California shop on Rodeo Drive in Beverly Hills, Los Angeles, or drive across the Golden Gate Bridge in San Francisco.

Mexico's white sand beaches, sunny weather, and gently lapping water draw millions of tourists each year. The Baja California Peninsula stretches 800 miles (1,300 km) along the Pacific Ocean. People also visit some of Mexico's cities, such as Oaxaca and Tijuana, to listen to traditional Mexican music, eat delicious dishes, and buy unique handmade Mexican crafts, such as carvings, dishes, and clothing.

Fast Facts

Each year, more than 2 million people visit the 1,815-foot (553-m) tall CN Tower in Toronto, Canada, to take in the view from the tallest tower in the world.

Near Quinta Roo, Mexico, stand some of the oldest buildings known to humans. The ancient city of Tulum was built in AD 564. The city was named Tulum, which means "wall," because its stone buildings are protected by a wall.

Everglades National Park in Florida is the only place in the world where both crocodiles and alligators live together.

The Maya created huge ceremonial structures where rituals and theater could take place. Some of these structures were built along Mexico's Yucatan Peninsula, where their ruins still exist today.

Industry

With an abundance of natural resources, it is no wonder that manufacturing, forestry, the service industry, and tourism are the largest industries in North America.

Forestry is important to North America. In British Columbia, thick forests produce lumber for the world's pulp and paper industry. Mahogany, which is used to make furniture, comes from the rain forests of Mexico.

Mining is another important industry in North America. Nickel mined in Canada, oil drilled in parts of southern United States and Mexico, and bauxite from the Caribbean are shipped to countries around the world.

Since North America is home to two of the most industrialized nations in the world, manufacturing is one of its vital industries. Factories in the United States and Canada produce vehicles, equipment, household appliances, computers, electronic equipment, and food products that are sold around the globe.

Fast Facts

Canada is home to more than 180 native tree species. More than one-third of the country's forests are used by the lumber industry.

Environmentalist groups work to protect Mexico's rain forests from the logging industry because so many of the trees growing in these regions are **endangered**.

While mining in North America is a multimillion dollar industry, some individuals still have independent mining operations.

More than 140,000 technicians, engineers, and scientists work in North American steel mills.

Goods and Services

The United States and Canada have healthy economies, with high industrial growth, low **inflation**, and low unemployment. Canada and Mexico are the United States' largest trading partners. Over the past 20 years, manufacturing and the export of petroleum, coffee, and ore have helped boost Mexico's economy.

The United States is one of the largest importers and exporters in the world. Vehicles, food products, chemicals, and equipment are some of the major exports shipped from the United States. Canada's main exports are vehicles, metal, lumber, chemicals, and food products.

In North America, most cars and trucks are built in the United States. Many vehicle manufacturers have plants in Mexico, too.

The Past

Indigenous Peoples

Native Americans live in different groupings throughout North America. Some examples of Native American groups are the Inuit, Iroquois, Cherokee, Blackfoot, and Navajo.

Archaeologists believe the first Native Americans arrived in North America between 10,000 and 25,000 years ago. They crossed a massive land bridge that connected the continent to Asia. From the far north, they spread out across the continent. As they moved, some groups developed their own customs, traditions, and languages. When the Europeans arrived between the 1400s and 1600s, many Native Americans died. Some fell ill with diseases brought by the Europeans. Others were enslaved and died in poor living conditions. Some were killed in battle.

Today, there are more than 2 million Native Americans living in the United States, and about 800,000 in Canada. In Mexico, many people are descended from the Aztec, who lived in Central and South America before the arrival of European explorers in the 1400s.

Fast Facts

The Seward Peninsula, Alaska, is home to the Bering Land Bridge National Preserve. The peninsula is part of the ancient land bridge crossed by the ancestors of Native Americans.

When Christopher Columbus reached the Americas, he believed he had landed in India. When he met the indigenous peoples, he called them *los indios,* which means "Indians."

The Serpent Mound in the state of Ohio is a burial mound built by the Adena, a Native American group who lived in the southern United States between 500 BC and AD 200.

In the 1800s, Northwest Coast Native Peoples, including the Haida, Tlingit, and Tsimshian of Alaska and British Columbia, carved figures and symbols into tall cedar poles. Some of these poles were used as doorways to houses or to honor former chiefs.

The Age of Exploration

The Vikings were the first-known European explorers to sail across the cold waters of the Atlantic Ocean to North America. More than 500 years later, Italian explorer Christopher Columbus landed on the continent in 1492. Other explorers from France, Portugal, and Spain soon followed.

Christopher Columbus made four trips to the Caribbean and South America between 1492 and 1504.

John Cabot explored the northeast coast of Canada and the United States in 1497. In 1534, a French explorer named Jacques Cartier reached Newfoundland, the Gulf of the St. Lawrence River, and the Gaspé Peninsula. He named this area New France.

While explorers from France and Great Britain searched for a passage from the Atlantic Ocean to the Pacific Ocean by way of northern North America, the Spanish searched for gold in the southern part of the continent. Juan Ponce de León, an explorer from Spain, discovered what is now Florida in 1513 while searching for riches. In 1539, Hernando de Soto discovered the Mississippi River. The Spanish built colonies in the Caribbean and Mexico.

Fast Facts

The Spanish searched for a mythical land that was made of gold. After they met the **Aztec** in Mexico, who had many goods made from gold, many other explorers came to the region in search of the mythical land.

Conquistador was the name given to the Spanish explorers who conquered parts of North and South America in the 1500s.

Jacques Cartier's attempt to colonize New France failed, but the good relationship he established with the Native American peoples in the region opened the way for the fur trade in North America, an industry that helped to establish Canada and the United States.

Early Settlers

Great Britain sent many explorers to North America, but it was not until 1606 that John Smith built the first successful **colony** in Jamestown, Virginia. Later, explorers, such as Samuel de Champlain, mapped the interior of Canada and the United States, and claimed land for France. The French claimed much of the land around the St. Lawrence River and north toward present-day Quebec, while the British ventured south into the area now known as the United States. The French continued their exploration of the Great Lakes and the Mississippi River.

Throughout the 1600s, the Spanish moved northward into the present-day United States. France claimed land to the south of New France, and Great Britain established colonies around Hudson Bay and along the eastern coast of North America.

On April 26, 1607, British settlers landed in Jamestown, Virginia. John Smith was chosen as one of the seven leaders of the new colony.

Between 1689 and 1760, Great Britain and France fought over the land in North America in four wars. The conflict ended in 1763, when the British defeated the French. The land in North America was divided between the Spanish and the British. Still, some British colonists wanted independence. In 1775, thirteen British colonies rebelled against Great Britain, and war erupted. In 1783, Great Britain gave these colonies their independence, and they became the United States. In 1867, present-day Canada was established.

Spanish explorer Hernán Cortés arrived in Mexico in 1519. With an army of about 200 Spanish soldiers and many indigenous peoples, Cortés battled against the ruling Aztec peoples. Though he had early success, Cortés and his army were forced to retreat. They returned in 1521 to conquer the Aztecs—claiming most parts of Mexico and Central America for Spain.

Fast Facts

John Smith was almost killed by a Native-American chief called Powhatan. Smith was saved by Powhatan's daughter, Pocahontas.

Samuel de Champlain is credited with founding the settlement of Stadacona in New France. This settlement is now known as Quebec City, the capital of the province of Quebec.

In the 1600s, a group of men known as the *coureur de bois*, or "forest runners," emerged in New France. These men knew the forests well and were hired by explorers to guide them through difficult areas.

On July 4, 1776, the Declaration of Independence was signed. This document proclaimed the American colonies free from British rule.

Mexico's emperor, Montezuma, welcomed Cortés and his army to his realm, but he was then taken hostage during the Spanish invasion. Montezuma was killed when his people revolted against the Spanish.

Culture

Population

More than 500 million people live in North America. It is home to some of the world's most populated cities, including Mexico City, New York City, and Los Angeles.

In 2004, there were nearly 300 million people living in the United States, more than 32 million in Canada, and about 105 million in Mexico. Most North Americans are descended from the British, French, or Spanish who colonized the continent. Both Canada and the United States are very multicultural and have become home to people from all parts of the world. Canada's population includes people of German, Italian, Polish, Ukrainian, Chinese, Dutch, and Scandinavian descent. The United States has large populations of people from Africa, Central and South America, Europe, and Asia, including Japan, China, the Philippines, Korea, and Vietnam. People of Native American descent live throughout the continent.

Many people move to North America in search of a better life for themselves and their families. Some also want safety from wars in their home country, or a place where they can practice their political or religious beliefs.

More than 8,100,000 people live in New York City.

Politics and Government

The history of each major country in North America is reflected in its politics and government. Although the countries have different government practices, each uses a system called democracy. In a democracy, the people of the country vote to elect a leader who is responsible for governing the country.

Within the democratic countries of North America, there are political parties. Political parties are groups of politicians who have similar beliefs about the way in which their countries should operate. Through elections, politicians from different parties win seats in government. This gives them power to vote on laws. The leader of the country is the person whose political party has won the most seats in an election.

The head of the United States government is the president. The president, vice president, House of Representatives, and the Senate are responsible for making and passing laws and running the country. In Canada, a prime minister leads the government. The prime minister works with the House of Commons and the Senate to run the country. A president is the head of the Mexican government. Other government bodies, including the Congress of the Union and The Supreme Court of Justice of the Nation, work together to run the country.

Fast Facts

Canada has a federal government that represents the entire country, and provincial and territorial governments that represent each of the country's ten provinces and three territories.

The United States is divided into fifty states, each of which is run by a governor. Each of Mexico's thirty-one states is also run by a governor.

The capital of Canada is Ottawa, Ontario. The capital of the United States is Washington, DC, and the capital of Mexico is Mexico City.

The Capitol of the United States serves as the seat of the U.S. Congress. The laws of the United States are made in this building, which sits on Capitol Hill in Washington, DC.

Cultural Groups

North America has a wide range of cultural groups, each of which contributes to the character of the land. Each culture living in North America has brought its language, religion, and traditions from its home country.

Most North Americans speak English. English is the official language of the United States. English and French are the official languages of Canada. Spanish is the official language of Mexico, and one of the most common languages spoken in the United States. In each country, many Native Americans still speak their native language. For example, many of the Inuit who live in Greenland, Canada, and the United States speak Inuktituk. In Mexico, some people also speak the Aztec language called Náhuatl.

Churches, synagogues, mosques, and temples are found throughout North America. Many people in Canada, the United States, and Mexico are **Christians.** Other religions practiced in North America include Islam, Judaism, Buddhism, and Hinduism. As well, many Native Americans have traditional forms of worship they pass down from generation to generation.

Work began on the Metropolitan Cathedral in Mexico City in 1573. In 1667, the incomplete cathedral opened. The two bell towers and central dome were finished in 1813.

Cultural celebrations reflect the backgrounds and beliefs of North America's many cultural communities. People celebrate religious holidays, including Christmas, Hanukkah, Eid, and Diwali. They also celebrate festivals that are popular in their home countries, such as Chinese New Year and Cinco de Mayo. On November 2, the people of Mexico celebrate El día de Los Muertos, or "Day of the Dead." During the celebration people put colorful toys, carvings, and crafts on the graves of their loved ones.

Many Native Peoples celebrate the Sun Dance, which is held at the beginning of summer. The Sun, which gives life, is a part of many Native beliefs. People dance, give thanks, and share a large meal. Some Sun Dance celebrations last as long as 12 days.

Carnaval is one of the most popular festivals in Latin American countries, including Mexico. Each year, people dress in costumes, hold parades, sing, play music, and enjoy a feast. Carnaval is much like the Mardi Gras celebrations held in the United States and the Quebec Winter Carnival in Canada. Each festival is part of a celebration that takes place prior to a Christian season called **Lent**.

Fast Facts

In Canada, about 25 percent of the population speaks French.

Potlatch is a ceremony shared by many Native Peoples from the Northwest. It consists of a large party with hundreds of guests, as well as a great deal of food, singing, and dancing.

Thanksgiving is a day for people in both the United States and Canada to give thanks for all they have received in the past year. The first Thanksgiving celebrations were harvest festivals in which settlers celebrated bountiful crops.

The Virgin of Guadalupe is Mexico's **patron saint**. Throughout Mexico, celebrations honoring the saint are held on December 1 each year. Colorful parades, traditional dress, music, and food are part of the festival.

Mexican Americans celebrate Cinco de Mayo, which means the fifth of May, with parades, dancing, and music. The celebrations are in honor of the Mexican defeat over the French in 1862.

Arts and Entertainment

North America is home to some of the most well-known artists, authors, musicians, actors, and entertainers in the world. The continent is also home to museums that hold artifacts from around the world, art galleries that hold paintings and sculptures by some of the world's most important artists, and theaters where all kinds of music and plays are performed.

The work of North American artists, including American painter Andy Warhol and Mexican artist Frida Khalo, is displayed at the Museum of Modern Art (MoMA) in New York City. The MoMA is one of the largest and most visited museums in North America. Another internationally known museum is the Smithsonian, located in Washington, DC. This museum is housed in several buildings. Each focuses on a specific area of interest, ranging from African art to natural history.

Some of the best-known celebrities in the world come from North America. Salma Hayek began her film career in a soap opera in Mexico. Today, she is an actress in Hollywood films. Jennifer Lopez is a well-known

Andy Warhol was known for using everyday objects, such as soup cans, as subjects for his art.

singer and actress who was born in New York to parents from Puerto Rico. Johnny Depp, Julia Stiles, Josh Hartnett, and Reese Witherspoon are just a few of the many American-born actors. Jim Carrey, Mike Myers, and Elisha Cuthbert are Canadian-born actors.

Books written in North America are translated into hundreds of languages and read around the world. Some authors, such as American John Steinbeck and Canadian Lucy Maud Montgomery, have written about life in their home country. Other authors, such as Cuban-American author Christina García, write about moving to a new country in North America and maintaining their culture and traditions.

Canadian author Margaret Atwood has written more than 35 internationally acclaimed works of fiction, poetry, and essays.

Fast Facts

In 1990, author Octavio Paz was the first Mexican to win the **Nobel Prize** in Literature.

In 2001, Jennifer Lopez's movie *The Wedding Planner* was the number one movie in the United States, while her CD *J-Lo* was the number one record. She was the first woman in history to have a top movie and CD in the same week.

The Group of Seven was a group of Canadian painters. Their work depicts the Canadian wilderness in a colorful and unique way.

Phillis Wheatley was the first African-American author published in the United States. Her collection of poems, *Poems on Various Subjects,* was published in 1773.

Jennifer Lopez has sold more than 35 million CDs worldwide.

Sports

People enjoy a variety of sports and activities in North America. They ski, snowboard, and hike its many mountains, swim in its rivers, lakes, and oceans, and cycle and walk through its beautiful parks and natural landscapes. Playing golf, soccer, football, ice hockey, and basketball are also popular activities.

Soccer is one of North America's most popular sports, especially in Mexico. The World Cup soccer championship is the largest and most popular soccer competition in the world. Mexico, Canada, and the United States all have teams that compete in this worldwide event.

Fast Facts

At the 2004 Summer Olympic Games in Athens, Greece, the United States won a total of 103 medals—more than any other participating country.

Although the game of baseball watched today began in the United States, archaeologists have found evidence that ancient peoples in Greece, Persia, and Egypt played games with bats and balls.

Mexico and the United States played against each other in the qualifying round of the 2006 World Cup. Mexico won the game by a score of 2 to 1.

Baseball, which is often called "America's Pastime," was invented in North America. In this game, two teams of nine players each attempt to get more players to complete a run around a diamond-shaped field. **Professional** baseball teams from Canada and the United States play in the Major League, but there are also professional leagues in Mexico.

One of the most popular sports in Canada is ice hockey. In this game, two teams compete to score more points by shooting a puck into a net. The National Hockey League (NHL) is the professional organization for this sport. NHL teams attract players from many parts of the world.

While living in the United States, a Canadian named James Naismith invented the game of basketball. Two teams play this game, as well. Players score points by throwing a ball through a hooped net located at each end of the basketball court.

Team USA and Team Canada often compete against each other at hockey's World Cup tournament.

Brain Teasers

1 Who are the Americas named after?

2 How many independent countries and nations are there in North America? What are the three largest?

3 How big is North America? How does it rank, or compare, to the world's other continents?

4 Which animal is one of Canada's national symbols?

5 Where is the only place in the world that crocodiles and alligators live together?

6	What is the name of the trade agreement made between Canada, the United States, and Mexico? What is important about the agreement?
7	How did the first inhabitants of North America arrive on the continent?
8	Who was John Smith? Who was Pocahontas?
9	What were the populations of Canada, the United States, and Mexico in 2004?
10	What is the Sun Dance?

For More Information

Books

Check the school or public library for more information about North America. The following books have useful information about the continent:

Alter, Judy. *Discovering North America's: Land, People, and Wildlife.* Berkeley Heights, NJ: Myreportlinks.com, 2004.

Nagle, Garrett. *North America.* London: Hodder Wayland, 2005.

Rau, Dana Meachan. *North America.* Chanhassen, MN: Child's World, 2003.

Web sites

You can also go online and have a look at the following Web sites:

CIA World Factbook
www.cia.gov/cia/publications/factbook

Canadian Children's Museum
www.civilization.ca

FirstGov for Kids
www.kids.gov

Mexico for Kids
www.elbalero.gob.mx/index_kids.html

Greenland Guide Index
www.greenland-guide.dk

Glossary

Algonquin dialect of the Ojibwa language spoken by Native Americans in eastern Canada

Aztec an ethnic group that ruled much of central and south Mexico prior to the Spanish conquest in 1521

bilingual able to read, write, and speak in two languages

boreal trees that grow in cold, northern climates and do not shed their leaves or needles

Christians people who believe in Jesus Christ's teachings

colonize to establish a settlement

colony a settlement ruled by a parent nation

deciduous trees that live in a variety of regions and shed their leaves in cold seasons

diverse having a large variety

endangered when so few of a species remain that they need protection in order to survive

environmentalist a person who works for the protection of the air, water, animals, plants, and other natural resources

equator an imaginary line at the center of the Earth that separates the Northern Hemisphere from the Southern Hemisphere

generate to create or produce

inflation a steady rise in the level of prices

Lent the 40 days before Easter

Nobel Prize an award for high achievement in chemistry, literature, physics, physiology or medicine, economics, and promoting world peace

patron saint a saint regarded as the special guardian of a person, group, or country

professional people who play sports for a living

SCUBA self-contained breathing apparatus

Index